The Yo
3 PEAK

C000047610

A 25 mile circular walk
scaling three of the highest peaks
in Yorkshire

*An essential guide to help you complete
the Yorkshire 3 peaks walk*

Brian Smailes

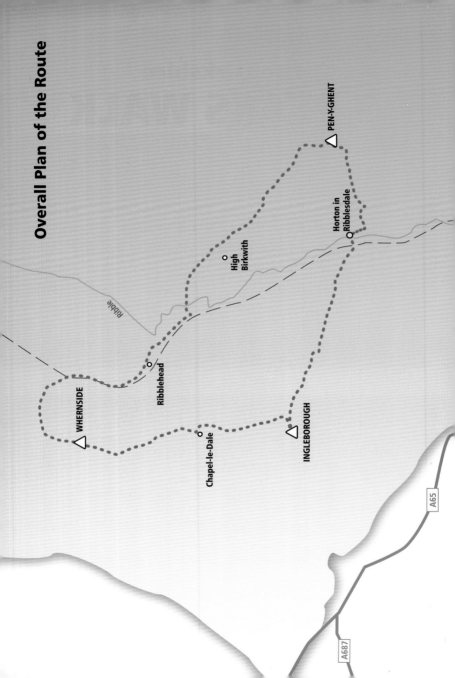

Overall Plan of the Route

PEN-Y-GHENT

Horton in
Ribblesdale

High
Birkwith

Ribble

WHERNSIDE

Ribblehead

Chapel-le-Dale

INGLEBOROUGH

A65

A687

Brian Smailes

Holds the record for the fastest 4 and 5 continuous crossings of the Lyke Wake Walk over the North York Moors. He completed the 210 miles over rough terrain on 5 crossings in June 1995, taking 85 hours and 50 minutes. In 2010, he completed his 55th crossing.

The 2009 expedition was to walk the GR20 over the mountains in Corsica. This was an extreme challenge but worthwhile. An expedition in 2008 took Brian to the jungles around Canaima in Venezuela, exploring on foot and by dugout canoe the tributaries of the Rio Carrao up to Angel Falls.

China's Great Wall expedition in 2007 involved walking sections in remote areas along the former borders of Mongolia. On a 2005 expedition, Brian walked the Inca Trail in Peru, visiting Lake Titticacca and Bolivia while in the area.

In August 2003 he walked from John O'Groats to Lands End, completing it in 34 days. In August 2001 he cycled from Lands End to John O`Groats, a journey of over 910 miles in 6 days 13 hours 18 minutes. This involved carrying food, clothing and tent, and was completed without support between both ends.

A further cycle ride, this time from John O'Groats to Lands End took place in July 2007 to complete the two way cycle crossing.

Another end to end walk is planned for 2012 with the challenge to complete it in 29 days.

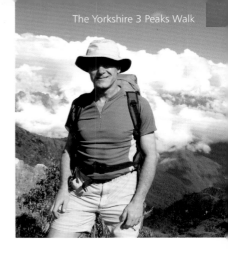

Brian has recently returned from an expedition to Chile and the mountains of Patagonia, exploring the flora and fauna and the glacial impact on the region.

Having travelled extensively throughout the UK, Europe and the Caribbean, Brian has also written international travel guides to enable the holidaymaker to access the world with ease and enjoy it as much as he does.

Long distance running, canoeing and sub aqua diving are other sports he enjoys, completing 26 marathons and canoeing the Caledonian Canal 3 times. Brian has dived all around the UK coastline as well as Thailand, Cuba, Venezuela, Egypt and Mexico.

Brian lives in Yorkshire and has walked the hills and dales throughout the County.

In compiling this 5th edition of The Yorkshire 3 Peaks Walk, the route still holds as much pleasure now as the first time he walked it.

Walk Guide Books

THE YORKSHIRE DALES TOP TEN
ISBN 978-0-9526900-5-4

THE LYKE WAKE WALK GUIDE
ISBN 978-1-903568-47-7

THE LYKE WAKE WALK SOUVENIR SKETCH MAP
ISBN 978-1-903568-58-3

THE YORKSHIRE 3 PEAKS WALK SKETCH MAP & ROUTE GUIDE
ISBN 978-1-903568-23-1

THE DERBYSHIRE TOP TEN
ISBN 978-1-903568-03-3

THE COMPLETE ISLE OF WIGHT COASTAL FOOTPATH
ISBN 978-1-903568-61-3

ISLE OF WIGHT, NORTH TO SOUTH – EAST TO WEST
ISBN 978-1-903568-07-1

THE NATIONAL 3 PEAKS WALK
ISBN 978 1-903568-53-8

THE SCOTTISH COAST TO COAST WALK
ISBN 978-0-9526900-8-5

20 WALKS AROUND GLEN NEVIS & FORT WILLIAM
ISBN 978-1-903568-05-7

JOHN O'GROATS TO LANDS END (Walking)
ISBN 978-1-903568-18-7

THE LANCASHIRE TRAIL

ISBN 978-1-903568-10-1

THE 1066 COUNTRY WALK

ISBN 978-1-903568-00-2

SHORT WALKS IN THE LAKE DISTRICT

ISBN 978-1-903568-20-0

WALK HADRIAN'S WALL

ISBN 978-1-903568-40-8

Tourist Guides

TOURIST GUIDE TO VARADERO, CUBA

ISBN 978-1-903568-08-8

EXPLORE – FORT WILLIAM & GLEN NEVIS

ISBN 978-1-903568-25-5

Cycling Guide

LANDS END TO JOHN O'GROATS

ISBN 978 1-903-568-59-0

Obtainable from bookshops or direct from the address below.
See web site for book details.

www.chall-pub.co.uk

THE YORKSHIRE 3 PEAKS WALK

ISBN 978-1-903568-62-0

Fifth Edition 2011

CHALLENGE PUBLICATIONS
7, EARLSMERE DRIVE, BARNSLEY. S71 5HH

Acknowledgements

It is with thanks to the following people for assistance, that this book has been published: -

Pam Smailes.

Jamie Mann.

Photography - Brian Smailes

Brian Smailes is identified as author of this book in accordance with Copyright Act 1988. No part of this publication may be reproduced by any means without prior permission in writing from the publisher.

First Published	**1994**
Second Edition	**2003**
Third Edition	**2004**
Fourth Edition	**2008**
Fifth Edition	**2011**

ISBN 978-1-903568-62-0

Published by Challenge Publications,
7, Earlsmere Drive, Ardsley, Barnsley, S71 5HH.
www.chall-pub.co.uk

The information recorded in this book is believed by the author to be correct at time of publication. No liabilities can be accepted for any inaccuracies found. Anyone using this guide should refer to the appropriate map in conjunction with this book.

The description or representation of a route used is not evidence of a right of way.

Contents

Page

Photographs 8

Illustrations 9

Foreword 10

Introduction 11

The Yorkshire Dales 12

Gradient Profile 13

Access to the Yorkshire Dales 14

Geology of the Area 16

Preparation 17

Equipment Selection 18

Boots & Blisters 20

Hypothermia 21

Top Tips for Completing the 3 Peaks .23

Safety System 24

Support Team 26

The Route in Detail with Grid References

- Pen-y-ghent 27

- Whernside 35

- Ingleborough 42

Escape Routes 49

Post Walk 51

Items of Interest on Route 52

Useful Information

Campsites 54

Accommodation Selection 54

Heights of Peaks 55

Walking Times 55

Distance to Nearest Main Villages 56

Other Notable Distances 56

Nearest Telephones on Route 57

Public Houses/Refreshments 57

National Park Centres 57

T.I.Cs in the Area 58

Useful Addresses/Telephone Numbers 58

Glossary of Words 60

Photographs

Front Cover – The author crossing the stile on Pen-y-gent Summit

1.	The start of the walk at Pen-ghent Café	9
2.	The turn off just before the church	11
3.	Pen-y-ghent in the distance with the path leading to it.	12
4.	One of the gates on the route to Pen-y-ghent	14
5.	The first steep ascent to the summit	15
6.	Good views on the ascent to the summit	17
7.	The descent from Pen-y-ghent with the path back to Horton turning off left	22
8.	Heading down to the first main beck to cross	25
9.	The beck which can have a lot more water after rain	30
10.	The next boggy section where you may have to navigate around	31
11.	The route showing the step stile with the path ascending by the wall	33
12.	Crossing the River Ribble after Nether Lodge	35
13.	Checkpoint one at Ribblehead Viaduct. The path to Whernside is mid right	38
14.	Whernside in the background with the route in the centre	39
15.	The path near Blea Moor signal box before the ascent to Whernside	41
16.	The start of the ascent beside Force Gill waterfall	45
17.	The slabbed path just before the final ascent onto Whernside	46
18.	On the summit of Whernside with Ingleborough in the background	48
19.	The descent from Whernside to the farm at Bruntscar (centre)	49
20.	Passing the farm at Bruntscar	50
21.	Crossing the fields just after leaving The Old Hill Inn	52
22.	The slabbed path to the base of Ingleborough	55
23.	The short steep ascent here in snow with the evening sun backdrop	56
24.	The final push to the summit of Ingleborough with the turn off right, back to Horton by the small vertical stone	57
25.	The 4 way wind shelter and 'trig' point on Ingleborough summit	58
26.	The route back to Horton in the valley by the white houses	59
27.	The lower ground by the limestone fields before reaching Horton	61
28.	The signpost before reaching Horton with Pen-y-ghent in the background	62
29.	Horton ahead showing the path which crosses the fields	64

Illustrations

Page

1. Overall Plan of the Route   2

2. The Body   19

3. Bird's Eye view of Pen-y-ghent showing the path   29
   onto and off the mountain

4. Bird's Eye view of Whernside   37

5. Bird's Eye view of Ingleborough   44

Please Note
The route section of this book is printed in a larger typeface to allow ease of reading whilst walking.

To assist in distinguishing each area, the headings, contents and captions are colour coded throughout:

Pen-y-ghent area	Ingleborough area
Whernside area	**General Information**

Photo 1. The start of the walk at Pen-ghent Café

Foreword

May we bid you a welcome to the Yorkshire Dales
and this Three Peaks guide by Brian G Smailes.

There is a lot of information for all to find
with the novice walker being kept in mind.

Before you start your journey up Pen-y-ghent,
just call at the café it is money well spent.

The proprietor there will gladly give you a talk
on his clocking system for The Three Peaks Walk.

It is a good system that I recommend you use,
the service is free so you've nothing to lose.

You just have to clock out when the walk you begin
and at the end of your journey you clock back in.

The simple thing that you have to do next
is to follow the route that's in Brian's text.

Having completed the walk, you may like to make
an attempt on The North York Moors Lyke Wake.

Finding the way shouldn't be hard for you
For Brian has wrote a guide on that too!

Geoff Whittaker

The Yorkshire 3 Peaks Walk presents a challenge to any walker, to scale three of the highest peaks in Yorkshire.

Situated in the Yorkshire Dales National Park, the 3 peaks of Pen-y-ghent, Whernside and Ingleborough nestle together around the village of Horton in Ribblesdale.

This all new 5th edition of The Yorkshire 3 Peaks walk is fully updated and is full of general information, sketch maps and directions to help you complete this walk. Read the following pages carefully then go and enjoy this exhilarating walk!

Introduction

Walkers travel from throughout Britain to climb the 3 peaks in this picturesque part of Yorkshire. The distance of 25 miles on this circular walk can be quite strenuous, but with some training and the careful selection of clothing and equipment to protect you from the elements, most people can complete it.

It usually takes between 9-13 hours to complete this walk. Some people run the course while others prefer a leisurely walk, with some staying overnight in a local B&B or camping on route.

All bearings are given as magnetic, 3° added to grid compass bearings from the map.

The Pen-y-ghent Café/Tourist Information Centre in Horton in Ribblesdale operates a unique safety system. When used correctly, it should ensure that nobody is unaccounted for at nightfall, and no walker is lost in the mountains without anyone knowing. More details further on.

An ever-increasing number of people use this walk as a 'training run' before attempting The National 3 Peaks Walk covering Ben Nevis, Scafell Pike and Snowdon. The 25 miles of this route will provide a good indication of fitness and stamina for the Nationals!

The route has suffered from erosion in parts, but careful preservation by staff and volunteers from various organisations have restored some areas to their former glory.

In the interests of the environment, it is recommended that walkers are in small groups on this walk and use only the defined paths to help prevent further erosion of this beautiful scenic area.

Photo 2. The turn off just before the church

The Yorkshire Dales

The Yorkshire Dales begins near Skipton in the south and is bordered by Settle, Ingleton with Sedberg to the west, Tan Hill to the north and Leyburn and Richmond to the east.

It is an area of natural beauty with mountains, limestone and gritstone fells, woodland and rivers.

There are numerous unspoilt villages throughout in typical Yorkshire style, displaying all the charm and elegance of a timeless age.

The area is a paradise for walkers and cyclists, where you can forget your car and enjoy the countryside. Those who prefer more active pastimes can visit the numerous potholes, caves and cliffs for climbing and exploring above and below ground.

The famous Settle-Carlisle railway crosses Ribblehead Viaduct (which you pass) on its journey. You may see train spotters there if a steam train is due, eager for a glimpse as it crosses the viaduct.

Television and film companies use the area frequently. Emmerdale and Calendar Girls were filmed near here, as are many others.

There are market days in most towns like Skipton (Mon. Wed. Fri. Sat.), Settle and Hawes (Tue), and Richmond (Sat) offering local and national products to discerning visitors from around the world.

Photo 3. Pen-y-ghent in the distance with the path leading to it.

Yorkshire 3 Peaks Walk Gradient Profile

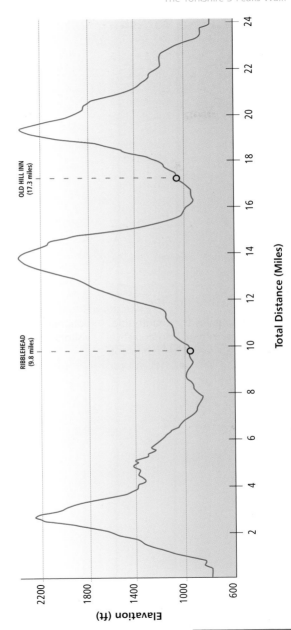

RIBBLEHEAD
(9.8 miles)

OLD HILL INN
(17.3 miles)

Elevation (ft)

Total Distance (Miles)

Access to the Yorkshire Dales

By Road:

The M6 passes Howgill Fells to the west, exit at J36 then follow the A65 towards Settle. The A1 passes to the east of Richmond and the main A610 from there leads onto the A684 into the dales. From the south, the dales can be reached from the M62, turning off to Bradford then Keighley and following the A629 to Skipton.

Bus/coach driving time from Bradford to Skipton is approximately 1 hour. National Coaches provide services to the larger towns e.g. Skipton and Richmond, where you can then connect with local transport to take you to your intended destination. Check with a T.I.C. for current coach times.

By Rail:

There are local stations in Skipton, Horton in Ribblesdale, Dent, Settle and Ribblehead. The southern dales area is covered by the Leeds-Skipton-Carlisle line, which passes over Ribblehead Viaduct, where you can exit at Horton in Ribblesdale for your 3 peaks walk. Timetables change, so please contact either the National Rail enquiries or T.I.C. for current times of trains.

Photo 4. One of the gates on the route to Pen-y-ghent

By Air:

There are two main airports covering the area, Leeds-Bradford and Manchester.

Visitors to the area are encouraged to travel by public transport or bicycle to help cut pollution and congestion in the dales.

Telephone numbers for T.I.Cs, coach, air and rail enquiries are given in the back of this book to help you to confidently plan your journey and walk.

Photo 5. The first steep ascent to the summit

The Geology of the Area

The Yorkshire Dales area is principally a limestone base, dating from the carboniferous period, although there is evidence below this of Ordovician and Silurian rock strata.

This limestone was formed when corals and sea creatures died, their shells thus creating this base. It took millions of years and numerous climatic changes to lay down this limestone layer. Further changes took place resulting in layers of sandstone, shale and mudstone being deposited through a glacial drift down the valleys.

To finish the geological strata of the area, a deposit of millstone grit was laid down in the tributaries of a river that flowed through the area on its journey to the sea. Some peaks have this deposit of millstone grit covering them, but the valleys gradually became covered with plants, trees and swamps, resulting in some coal deposits being found in the north of the area.

When rain, frost and sun 'weathers' the limestone, it becomes scarred with cracks and fissures, worn from the rock above and below ground, resulting in the many potholes in the area.

Around the Ingleborough plateau in particular, you can see the fields of limestone outcrops with their fissures and gullies like spiders webs, entrapping the careless feet of any walker who ventures over it in a casual manner.

Walking the 3 peaks will involve navigating between these limestone outcrops and over rock formations, so take care. I am sure you will find these geological structures of the area fascinating to see, as I still do after many visits.

Preparation

When preparing for this walk, you have to remember there are a lot of ascents and descents, therefore knees and ankles should be in good working order before you leave.

Although the distance is only 25 miles, any walker attempting this walk needs to be reasonably fit, so training before the walk is recommended. Start by walking short distances two – three months before the event then gradually increase your distance walked, ensuring you incorporate some hills into your training routes. Build up to 20 miles if possible during training incorporating rock, grass and moorland terrain. This training should ensure you are reasonably fit to complete the 3 peaks.

Other types of fitness training e.g. cycling, keep fit sessions, jogging and swimming will all increase your overall fitness and stamina

and help to prepare you for this undulating course.

Training in the use of basic map and compass work will be helpful, especially if the peaks are covered in cloud as often happens in bad weather.

Consuming high-energy food before and during the walk is most beneficial. Food with a high level of carbohydrate such as rice, pasta, potato, banana, malt loaf and milk, will help to build up your energy reserves before the walk. While walking, glucose based sweets, apples and Kendal mint cake will all help to supply your body with extra energy, as will isotonic drinks.

Finally, from past experience, those who do some type of exercise before the walk and do not drink or smoke heavily, usually complete the walk. Those who do nothing and drive from A to B do not!

Photo 6. Good views on the ascent to the summit

Equipment Selection

When considering equipment and clothing for this walk, you must remember that it may be a calm, still, and what seems like a nice day in Horton in Ribblesdale but nearing the summit of any mountain it can be cold and very windy with low cloud. Often it is the wind chill factor that causes problems for walkers. With this in mind, the following suggested list of items should help you to both complete the walk and stay warm, dry and hopefully injury free.

- ❏ Compass and guide book
- ❏ Walking boots/fell boots
- ❏ Walking socks including 2 spare sets
- ❏ Walking trousers (no jeans)
- ❏ Warm upper body clothing (in layers),
- ❏ Spare clothing
- ❏ Gloves, hat
- ❏ Torch with spare bulb and batteries
- ❏ Whistle, note paper and pencil
- ❏ Toilet paper
- ❏ Survival bag
- ❏ Basic first aid kit including plasters and Vaseline
- ❏ Fleece/waterproof fabric outer jacket/cagoule, over trousers
- ❏ Day rucksack
- ❏ Food, plastic drinks bottle
- ❏ Camera
- ❏ Map of the area O.S. Explorer OL2 Yorkshire Dales.

Use this as a checklist before you leave. In addition to the above items, a complete change of clothes should be available at the campsite/bed and breakfast or in your car at Horton in Ribblesdale ready for when you return.

The Body

Should be kept warm. Build clothes up in layers with wind/waterproofs on top.

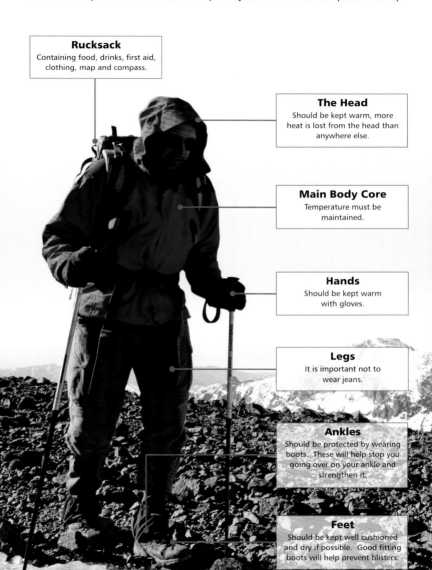

Rucksack
Containing food, drinks, first aid, clothing, map and compass.

The Head
Should be kept warm, more heat is lost from the head than anywhere else.

Main Body Core
Temperature must be maintained.

Hands
Should be kept warm with gloves.

Legs
It is important not to wear jeans.

Ankles
Should be protected by wearing boots. These will help stop you going over on your ankle and strengthen it.

Feet
Should be kept well cushioned and dry if possible. Good fitting boots will help prevent blisters.

Boots & Blisters

Two of the most important things on this walk are your feet and boots. If your feet hurt or you suffer with bad blisters, then you may not complete the walk. Boots need to be big enough to fit comfortably but not too big so your feet move around inside whilst walking. Remember to fit the boots with the socks you will be wearing when walking.

Sprinkle a liberal quantity of foot powder on your feet and in the socks. Put powder into your boots and on the outside of your socks, then put your boots on making sure your feet fit snugly into them. This method has helped many people to keep their feet not only dry and fresh throughout but more importantly blister free.

Change socks as often as you feel you need to. Doing this will refresh your feet and provide cushioning. If you feel any warm spots on your feet or toes, do not wait until a blister has formed, it is too late then. Change socks, sprinkle foot powder on or put a plaster on.

Remember to cut your toenails short before you leave home so you don't get any undue pressure on your toes whilst walking or descending hills, which will result in black and painful toe nails or the loss of them!

Hypothermia

Hypothermia is caused when the body core temperature falls below 35ºC. If a walker is not properly prepared for the conditions or the clothing worn is not satisfactory, then a combination of the cold, wet, exhaustion and the wind chill factor can give a walker hypothermia.

When you stop walking for a while, you quickly get cold. To combat this, put another layer on, zip up and put gloves and hat on.

The Signs and Symptoms in Descending Order: -

- *Shivering*
- *Cold, pale and dry skin*
- *Low body temperature*
- *Irrational behaviour*
- *A gradual slip into unconsciousness*
- *Pulse and respiratory rate slow*
- *Difficulty in detecting breathing and pulse when unconscious*
- *Death*

Ways of Preventing Hypothermia

- Build up body clothing in thin layers, adding on or taking off as necessary.
- Have suitable wind/waterproofs with you.
- Take some food/hot drink or boiled sweets, which produce energy and heat during digestion.
- Wear a balaclava/woolly hat to insulate the head, and some gloves.
- Shelter out of the wind.
- Take a survival bag and if conditions dictate, use it.

In any type of emergency/accident situation it is always advisable to come off the higher ground as soon as possible especially in low cloud, snow or other bad conditions. The temperature difference between a valley and the high ground can be several degrees.

Photo 7. The descent from Pen-y-ghent with the path back to Horton turning off left

(label in image: Pile of stones)

Treatment for Hypothermia

- Provide extra clothing and shelter from the elements.

- Bodily warmth of others helps in a gradual warming.

- If well enough come down into a warmer sheltered area.

- Give hot, sweet drinks if conscious.

- Give chocolate or sweets if the patient can still take food.

- The casualty should be placed so that the head is slightly lower than the body.

DO NOT *rub the skin or use a hot water bottle as this can cause a surge of blood from the central body core to the surface, this could prove fatal.*

Alcohol should not be consumed on any walk and should not be given to anyone who has hypothermia. The body temperature will be lowered as well as giving a false sense of security.

Top Tips for Completing the 3 Peaks

- Prepare and train before the walk. Those who do some training usually succeed, those who do not, don't succeed.

- Take and wear the right walking clothing. This includes boots, waterproof jacket and trousers, (see equipment list). No jeans or high heels!

- Carry at least two spare pairs of walking socks and change them between each mountain. This will help to revive your feet and give them new life.

- Eat little and often. Doing this will give a constant supply and release of energy to the body.

- Drink regularly. If the body becomes dehydrated, you will lose energy fast.

- Carry a map and compass with you and know how to use them.

- Ensure you have emergency and first aid items with you including torch, survival bag, first aid kit and blister plasters.

- If you feel a blister forming or a warm spot on your feet, do not wait until the blister has formed. Stop and put a plaster on before it is too late. Look after your feet and they will look after you!

- Cut toenails short before you leave home.

- Carry only items you need for ascending each mountain and no more. Remember you have to walk up and down 3 mountains. Grams turn into kilograms, ounces into pounds every time you put something more into your rucksack.

- Leave details of your route and approximate return time with the support team/B&B/friends or in the café in Horton by using their safety system.

- If walking at night, ensure you carry spare batteries and bulb. Do not be left in darkness.

- On reaching the summit of each peak, only stay as long as necessary. If you feel cold then leave the summit and descend to lower ground where it is usually warmer.

Safety System

Pen-y-ghent Café operates a unique safety system. Before you leave Horton in Ribblesdale, you can register details of your intending walk or other activity at the café. There is a card to complete and the following details are required:

- Name
- Home Address
- Tel. No.
- Time of departure
- Reg. No. of your vehicle
- Where parked
- Local/Holiday address if not returning home tonight

A multiple or 'early bird' booking out sheet is available, ask in the café.

After completing the card there is a clock card machine to register your start time. Hand the card in at the counter before leaving. As soon as you return to Horton in Ribblesdale, you should go back to the café and ask for your card to 'clock back in'. This is extremely important, because if you do not call back in a reasonable time, then you could be reported missing and a search initiated.

Following this procedure is simple and there is **no charge for this service.** There are some exceptions to the above procedure as follows:

- If you leave before the café opens, you can put all the above details on a piece of paper and put through the letterbox.

- The safety service operates every weekend. It also operates on some weekdays with prior arrangement except Tuesdays when the café is closed.

- The café is normally open Wed to Mon 9am – 5.30pm (with seasonal variations), but if any walker has not returned, the café will stay open until all walkers are accounted for. The latest time you can depart is 9am if you are using the safety service.

Note: At the time of printing this book in May 2011, the safety system mentioned above has been temporarily suspended. It is hoped to reinstate it at some point in the future.

It is still possible to register to join the 3 Peaks of Yorkshire Club. Further details in the cafe.

Pen-y-ghent Café is fully networked with the English Tourist Board (tourist information centre) and can assist with accommodation, parking advice and general information.

Should your return be delayed for any reason and you cannot 'clock back in', then you should telephone 01729 860333 (café) to avoid a search being initiated.

Those who use the safety system and complete the 3 Peaks Walk within a 12-hour period are eligible to join the 3 Peaks of Yorkshire Club and wear the exclusive badge and tie.

Membership is by invitation only, and by complying with the safety rules. Use the system wisely and be assured that at least someone knows you are out in wild country and have not yet returned.

Photo 8. Heading down to the first main beck to cross

Support Team

Some people attempt this 3 peaks walk using a support team who meet them at each of the two checkpoints. The two checkpoints are Ribblehead Viaduct at GR. 765793, which is 5.8 miles (9.3 km) from Horton, and nearby The Old Hill Inn at GR. 743776 (park in layby), which is 1.8 miles (2.9 km) from Ribblehead by road.

Walkers should be aware of the distance and approximate walking times between checkpoints and decide whether they can walk to the next checkpoint or retire honourably at the one they are at.

A good support team will give verbal encouragement as well as hot food and drinks to the walkers. When arriving at a checkpoint, walkers should not have to wait too long for food and drinks. These should be ready when the walkers arrive. Too long spent at a checkpoint will result in walkers feeling stiff and tired. As the walk progresses, the time spent at a checkpoint becomes more critical as the body becomes stiffer.

A good safety precaution is for the support team to operate a check in system at each checkpoint where walkers report in to a nominated person on arrival. Taking this precaution should ensure no walker has gone astray between checkpoints.

Members of any support team should have some knowledge of first aid and should be able to recognise the symptoms of exposure. They should be aware of the location of the nearest telephones for emergency and be experienced map readers and fit walkers, prepared to give assistance to any of the walkers in an accident/emergency situation. They should keep a spare rucksack ready to take with them in emergency with the following inside: -

- Map
- Compass
- Whistle
- Survival Bag
- Notepad/Pencil
- Spare Clothing
- First Aid Kit
- Sleeping Bag
- Emergency Food/drink
- Torch *(plus spare bulb/batteries)*
- Mobile Telephone *(may not function in mountainous areas)*.

It may be decided that the best course of action is to go straight to the aid of a walker rather than contact the mountain rescue team initially. Any potential risks to either the injured or lost walker or the rescuer should be carefully considered before deciding your course of action.

The Route in Detail

Pen-y-ghent

Grid References for Horton - Pen-y-gent - Ribblehead

Horton in Ribblesdale start	**GR.SD** 808725
	810722
	812722
	817723
	819724
	830727
	836728
	838733
Pen-y-ghent Summit	839734
	838735
Turn off back to Horton	839742
	836744
	830748
	824751
	820754
	813758
	806766
	803772
	796777
	785780
	780780
	777783
Ribblehead Viaduct	765793

Grid references are given here and throughout the route description particularly to assist walkers who have a GPS system to identify with places on route.

Pen-y-ghent Gradient Profile

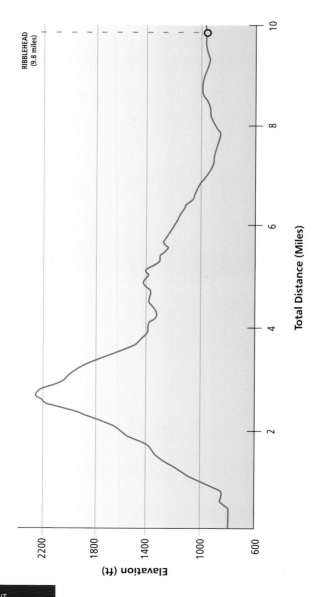

Horton in Ribblesdale

Pen-y-ghent

To Ribblehead

Return route to Horton

Horton – Pen-y-ghent - Ribblehead Route

Turn right out of the car park (charge) in Horton in Ribblesdale, GR. SD 808725 and proceed to the Pen-y-ghent Café/Tourist Information Centre (photo1), which is about 50m along the road on your right. After using the free safety service in the shop, turn right and continue along towards the church, on the opposite side of the road, you will see the track that descends from Pen-y-ghent and emerges in Horton opposite the café. This is useful if you decide only to walk one mountain and return to Horton, or you are using the new alternative route section. Continuing along the road, you

should see the church at the south end of the village. You will pass Holme Farm campsite on your right where you cross the road.

Just past the campsite there is a small field on the opposite side with a narrow wooden gate, just before the church, (photo 2), turn left here on a narrow path across the field. The church is a short distance away now to your right. Proceed through the next two small gates ahead of you then turn left onto a metalled road. You will see a bridge over the stream about 35m further on. Cross over the footbridge and turn left onto a

Photo 9. The beck which can have a lot more water after rain

metalled road, passing the local school.

Continue on the metalled road for 700m, keeping the stream on your left until you come to a farm at Brackenbottom GR. SD 817723 where there is a signpost pointing to 'Pen-y-ghent summit 1¾ miles' Turn left here through a gate, keeping close by a stone wall. The grass path now ascends steeply for just over 2km to the gate on the ridge at the base of Pen-y-ghent, and there are many ruts in the worn path.

Go through another gate further up before you arrive at stone steps in the wall ahead of you and Pen-y-ghent appears directly ahead (photo 3). Walk through another gate on the way up (photo 4), and continue ascending over two large stone outcrops, generally keeping alongside the stone wall in the direction of Pen-y-ghent. This area is known as Brackenbottom Scar. Looking behind, you can see Ingleborough in the distance with Horton in the valley and the quarry behind. Nearing the base of Pen-y-ghent you may see a gate in the wall on the ridge ahead. As you continue to ascend steeply you climb a flight of man made stone steps, laid to combat footpath erosion. Going through the gate on the ridge, you join the Pennine Way where you now have a view of the east side of Pen-yghent. This area is an important site for ground nesting birds.

Photo 10. The next boggy section where you may have to navigate around

Just as you go through the gate, there is a new stone path on the left ascending to the summit, which is steep and care should be taken (photo 5). The general compass bearing from the gate to ascend the path in low cloud is 17°M. As you approach the higher slopes (photo 6), there are some steep steps up the large rock outcrop. The path starts to flatten out before the final short ascent to the summit and the triangulation pillar, 'trig' point number S5776. Enjoy the view in all directions, weather permitting. There are also good views of Ingleborough to the west and Whernside to the NNW.

Near the triangulation pillar on the summit, there are two sets of steps over the stone wall, go over and you should see your path going downhill bearing 340°M from the stile. Follow the path for 300m then it bears right, still descending a further 600m to a pile of stones (photo 7). **N.B.** This path is reasonably obvious, although care should be taken especially in low visibility.

At this pile of stones, the path on your left leads back to Horton in Ribblesdale (photo 7), and is part of the Pennine Way. The pile of stones marks the turning. It is useful if you decide to climb only one mountain then return to Horton. Returning by this path,

you emerge nearby the café in Horton.

This route described is the traditional route towards Ribblehead, but there are several sections which are boggy as mentioned in the next three paragraphs. There is an alternative route of approximately 4.8km which can be used, starting at the pile of stones in the previous paragraph.

Alternative section
From the pile of stones, turn left to descend an obvious path for 1.9km to a gate. Go through and initially bear 289°M, heading towards Whitber Hill (420m). Now take a general bearing of 310°M from Whitber Hill towards Sell Gill Hill.

Once on Sell Gill Hill, turn west for 400m towards the Pennine Way on general bearing of 288°M, following the worn path. Emerging on the Pennine Way (track) at GR. SD 810749, head north on the Pennine Way for 1.3km before crossing some stone steps on your left over a wall at GR. SD 810761 (photo 11) then ascending the hillside by the wall as shown in photo 11. You are now back on the main route heading in the direction of Dismal Hill. **This can be picked up on page 34.**

After passing this path on your left, continue on the main route straight ahead by the pile of stones on the main descending grass path bearing 310°M from the junction at GR. SD 838742. The path veers left for a short distance then appears to run parallel with the path that leads back to Horton. The paths are approx. 200m apart. The worn grass path in the distance ahead takes you to Horton Moor, leading to Ribblehead, which you may see in the distance.

Following the path you soon arrive at a wet and boggy section. After crossing this and a small brook beyond, there is a stone wall further ahead. Go through a gate and cross a stream (which may be dried out during summer (photos 8, 9). Cross a ladder stile then a wider stream known as Hull Pot Beck. Look for the worn grass path at all times and for Ribblehead Viaduct in the distance ahead.

After crossing the stream, you now cross Todber Moss at GR. SD 824751 then over numerous undulating small hillsides and the main area of natural springs (photo 10). All this area is usually very wet, even in summer, so navigate over it and the numerous ditches, gullies and dykes carefully for this 550m stretch. This area is known as Black Dub Moss at GR. SD 819754.

Go through a kissing gate before you come to a stone

Photo 11. The route showing the step stile with the path ascending by the wall

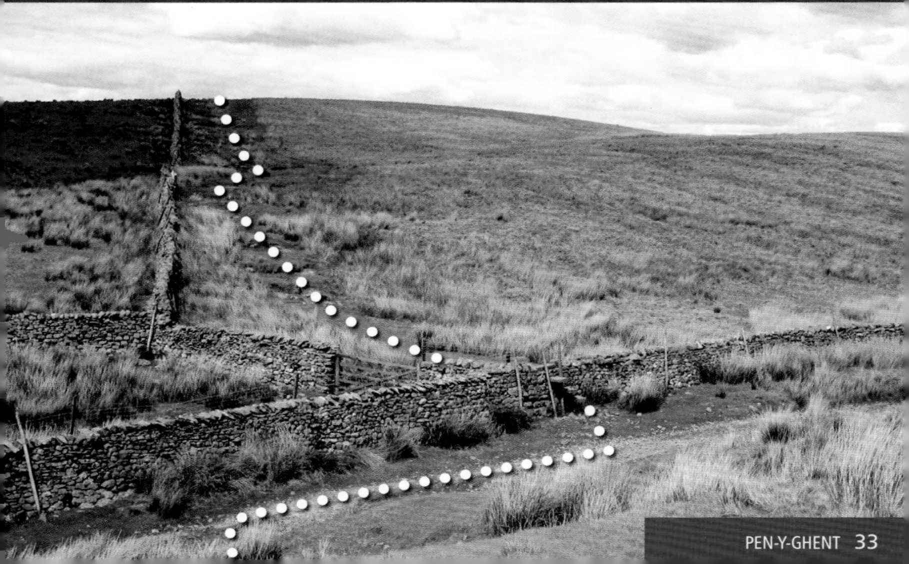

wall and farm gate ahead, but walk 30m to your right to **cross some stone steps over the wall (photo 11)**. Keep a stone wall now on your left as you ascend over the small hills still walking in the general direction of Ribblehead viaduct. It is undulating for another mile, with good views all around as you cross the Pennine Way. Go alongside the stone wall in front of you, then bear left across a grass field keeping the limestone rock pavement on your left. Go through an opening in a stone wall. The path turns to gravel and grass before crossing a narrow access road which leads to a farm on your right. There is a wood on your left, with Dismal Hill 300m to your right at GR. SD 806771.

After crossing this road go down a narrow path, crossing a stream then ascend back up again still heading towards Ribblehead in the same direction. Cross a stone step stile by a gate and follow a rutted farm track. You are now walking on part of The Ribble Way. Keep a stone wall on your left and as the path bends round to the left, bear right across the grass by the side of the wall.

Cross a stile at the side of a gate, following the undulating path, which is good in parts before it becomes a farm track. You may see Nether Lodge Farm in the far distance with Ribblehead Viaduct behind. Follow the path round and approaching the farmhouse, cross the stream over the hump back footbridge then go through the small gate, bearing left round the far side of the farmhouse.

You emerge at the far side on a good flat farm access road turn right on it and walk for 800m following the signpost pointing to Ribblehead. Cross a cattle grid then pass over a bridge which spans the upper reaches of the River Ribble (photo 12).

After 350m you start to ascend on a winding path to pass Lodge Hall, an impressive 17th century house. Just as you pass the house you walk on the tarmac access road. Follow this narrow road up to the main B6479 road. Cross the cattle grid there then turn right, walking for 1 mile (1.7 km) to the junction at Ribblehead Viaduct at GR. SD 765793.

This is where many people stop for a break and use this place as checkpoint 1. At the junction there is a sign pointing to Ingleton to your left. You walk straight across by the sign, heading towards the far end of the viaduct (photo 13), which has 24 arches.

Whernside

Grid References for Ribblehead - Whernside - Old Hill Inn

Ribblehead Viaduct	**GR.SD**	765793
		760795
		758806
Aquaduct		761816
		757824
		745826
Whernside Summit		738814
		735801
		739791
		740790
		743782
The Old Hill Inn		743776

Grid references are given here and throughout the route description particularly to assist walkers who have a GPS system to identify with places on route.

Photo 12. Crossing the River Ribble after Nether Lodge

Whernside Gradient Profile

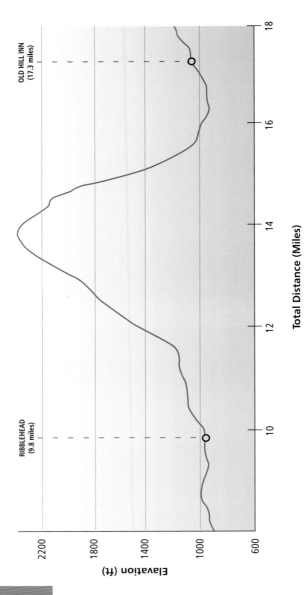

Elevation (ft)

Total Distance (Miles)

RIBBLEHEAD
(9.8 miles)

OLD HILL INN
(17.3 miles)

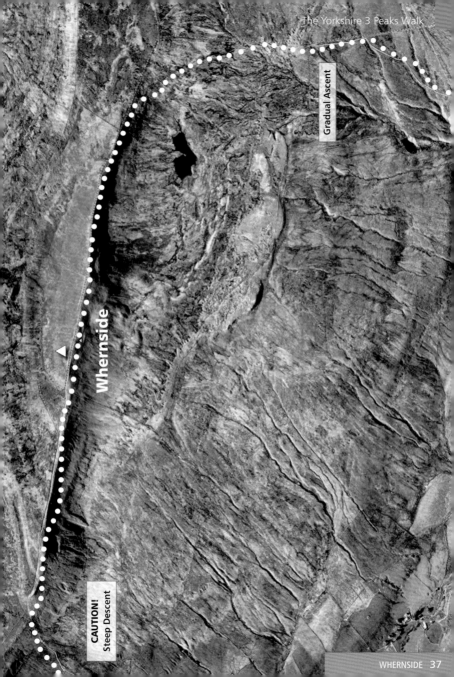

Gradual Ascent

Whernside

CAUTION!
Steep Descent

Ribblehead – Whernside - Old Hill Inn Route

At the junction there is a stream and often a refreshment van and it is a popular picnic spot, GR. SD 765793. Cross the road and carry on towards the viaduct keeping to the right of it and following the path to the far end before turning right to ascend a flight of stone steps up the short hillside with a stone wall on your left (photo 14) at GR. SD 758798. The Settle/Carlisle railway is parallel with your path as you now walk to Blea Moor signal box (photo 15) on the obvious path.

Your path turns to shale chippings as you proceed around the eatern side of Whernside. Go through a gate and continue on this undulating path for 800m to pass Blea Moor signal box and the renovated old railway house. This next section takes you over two small brooks (which may be dry) and the path is very stony and uneven. You cross a wide stream that is littered with stones but easily passable. There is a small footbridge if the stream is not passable This area is known as Blue Clay Ridge.

Photo 13. Checkpoint one at Ribblehead Viaduct. The path to Whernside is mid right

Nearing a stone wall continue on the path, which soon passes between two stone walls and crosses the railway line. Walk around the picturesque aqueduct at GR. SD 761816 then start to ascend. You will see the path, which you need to take, ahead of you. A signpost nearby states 'V.W. Dentdale 4 miles' in your direction of travel.

On your left you should see Force Gill (waterfall). Go over a stile, you start to walk anti-clockwise up Whernside ascending Slack Hill (photo 16). About halfway up there is a stile on your left over a wire fence. Cross and you are now ascending towards the summit on an obvious path. The bearing from the stile there is 311°M. The area around here can be boggy so stay on the stone slabbed path as you ascend and your feet should remain dry (photo 17). The slabbed path takes you directly to the summit of Whernside, passing over Grain Ings on route. On approaching the summit (photo 18), Pen-y-ghent can be seen off to your left and Ingleborough straight ahead.

Photo 14. Whernside in the background with the route in the centre

Below Whernside there is Greensett Tarn, which looks inviting on a hot day. On the summit on a clear day you can see Morecambe Bay to your right and the mountains of the Lake District to your extreme right.

On the summit is a 'trig' point just over the wall. Continue from the summit on the same path bearing 197°M from the main path again near the 'trig' point. The limestone plateau that surrounds Ingleborough can be clearly seen. You descend two short steep slopes, which are stony and uneven. Follow the stone wall gradually descending along for 1.2 km from the summit, then the path turns left away from the summit to descend steeply on bearing 159°M at GR. SD 734802, towards Bruntscar.

When taking this new path, extreme care should be taken, as the descending path down is stony, uneven and can be dangerous for about 80m, especially in wet weather. One slip could send you rolling down the hill. Further down, the path becomes gravel/stone and easier to walk on, as you make the gradual descent (photo 19) to the valley and farms on the way.

Go through two gates on the way down before turning right between old farm buildings, then after a short distance turn left at GR. SD 739790 to pass another farm 100m further at Bruntscar (photo 20). Look for the direction sign and arrow on the corner. There is a metalled access road now to walk along, and 500m ahead, a wood and ancient settlement at GR. SD 742784.

This narrow access road takes you past another farm building further on (with a snack bar open daytime during summer) on Philpin Lane and soon leads to the main road. Turn left at the main road and a short distance ahead you come to the Old Hill Inn at GR. SD 743776. This area is known as Chapel le Dale and is checkpoint 2.

Photo 15. The path near Blea Moor signal box before the ascent to Whernside

Ingleborough

Grid References for Old Hill Inn – Ingleborough - Horton in Ribblesdale

The Old Hill Inn	**GR.SD** 743776
	744777
	745772
	743763
Base of Ingleborough	747750
Ingleborough Summit	741746
	745747
	762740
Signpost in field approaching Horton	778735
	792731
	798729
	805726
Horton in Ribblesdale Near the Station	804726
Horton in Ribblesdale Car Park Finish	808725

Grid references are given here and throughout the route description particularly to assist walkers who have a GPS system to identify with places on route.

Ingleborough Gradient Profile

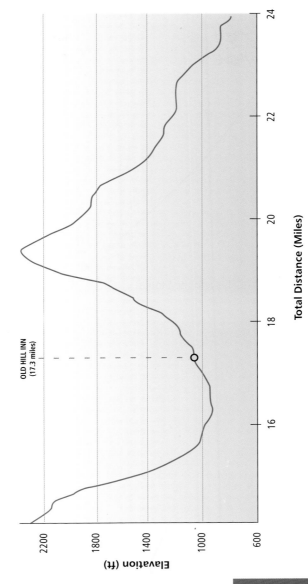

OLD HILL INN
(17.3 miles)

Elevation (ft)

2200 1800 1400 1000 600

16   18   20   22   24

Total Distance (Miles)

To Horton

Summit

Old Hill Inn – Ingleborough
- Horton in Ribblesdale Route

Leaving The Old Hill Inn, there is a small stile just above it on your right, hidden by two trees. Cross the stile and the field at the far side at GR. SD 745776. Turn right through the first farm gate on the right then cross several fields general bearing 210°M from the farm gate (photo 21) in the general direction of Ingleborough. The path is fairly obvious here. On your left side as you proceed you pass numerous limestone escarpments. The stone-chipping path a short distance further takes you through an area of limestone outcrops.

You pass a large pit or disused quarry on your left as you approach the base of Ingleborough. This is called Braithwaite Wife Hole GR. SD 745763. Continue on the path to a stone wall. Go through a gate onto a stone slabbed path (photo 22) which you walk on to the base of Ingleborough. This area is known as Humphrey Bottom, GR. SD 746752.

At the base of Ingleborough

Photo 16. The start of the ascent to the right of Force Gill waterfall

Photo 17. The slabbed path just before the final ascent onto Whernside

you should see a stepped path rising steeply up to the summit (photo 23) alongside a narrow stream and wall. This zigzag path is very steep so extra care needs to be taken, GR. SD 747749. Nearing the summit a signpost states 'National Nature Reserve' and 'Welcome to Ingleborough'.

Go through a kissing gate and you have your last short steep climb to the summit. **At the top of the steps, on your left, is the path you need, to take for your return to Horton in Ribblesdale, GR. SD 745747, marked by an upright stone (photo 24). You must ensure you do not miss this path.** Continue up the steep rocky outcrop to two piles of stones on the summit, with a 4-way wind shelter in view directly ahead (photo 25).

Ingleborough summit has a flat rocky plateau with a 'trig' point near the 4-way wind shelter. On the top of it is a plaque depicting the views in each direction. In low cloud or if disorientated, a compass bearing of 73°M from the 'trig' point should take you back to the path you

ascended. Retrace your steps now to the upright stone you passed on the ascent (photo 24), which marks the path back to Horton (mentioned in the last paragraph). Turn right at the stone on a bearing 100°M and descend on a steep path over Simon Fell Breast. Horton is now in the valley below with a view of Pen-y-ghent behind (photo 26).

Descending the hillside towards Horton, there are 4 gates to go through. Reaching the lower slopes, you walk on a descending grass path (photo 27). A sign pointing to Horton is just past it followed by a large limestone outcrop at GR. SD 773737. Your path runs between the limestone and undulating small hills.

Continue in a straight line towards Horton passing another signpost stating 'Horton 1½ miles' (experience says it could be further photo 28).

You are soon walking on a stony path where an opening through a stone wall leads to a large expanse of limestone rock. This area is known as Sulber Nick at

GR. SD 784733. Pick your path out carefully as you walk. The limestone rock diminishes as you near Horton and there are now fields, usually with animals in. The general bearing on the path back to Horton from where the limestone finishes and the fields begin is 117°M. Take extra care now for this final section of open fields can be the hardest to navigate over if descending in the dark (photo 29).

Cross the fields initially following the cairns or yellow marker sticks on a narrow, undulating path with stiles or gates in the stone walls. You will see a small tarn below the quarry. Continue to look for the worn path as you ascend to approach the railway line, go through a gate where you see a sign 'Horton in Ribblesdale' at the small station at GR. SD 804726. Cross the line with care and continue down the path and along the road in front towards the car park in the village.

There is a small bridge over the river on your right at the far end just before the Crown Hotel. Go over this and you are back in the car park. Return to the café and 'clock back in'. You are now free to partake of refreshment in a local hostelry and congratulate yourself on completing:

The Yorkshire 3 Peaks Walk!

Photo 18. On the summit of Whernside with Ingleborough in the background

Escape Routes

When climbing any peak, accidents can happen or cloud can descend quickly causing problems for unwary walkers. You may find your intended route is hard to find or you are heading into bad weather. In this situation you have a choice, retrace your steps back to safe ground (you will need to know where you have been) or go forward using a compass if necessary. **N.B.** it is good practice to sight compass and map before entering fog or poor visibility.

Alternatively you can use an escape route, which is designed to give you the quickest route back to a safe area, though not necessarily back to your intended destination.

The following 3 escape routes can be used as the quickest route down from the summit of the 3 peaks.

Pen-y-ghent GR. 839734

The shortest route from Pen-y-ghent summit to the nearest road at GR. 842714 is S.S.W. from the summit bearing 215°M on the Pennine Way then turning in a south-easterly direction after 1800m on bearing 113°M for a further 1000m.

Whernside GR. 738814

The shortest route from Whernside summit to the nearest road at GR. 722818 is in a westerly direction bearing 279°M from the 'trig' point on the summit. Follow a path for 900m descending, then walk for 150m on bearing 346°M. Now take a bearing of 282°M following a wall for 1150m down to the road.

Photo 19. The descent from Whernside to the farm at Bruntscar (centre)

Ingleborough GR. 741745

The shortest route to a road at a lower level is to The Old Hill Inn at GR. 743776. From the summit 'trig' Point bear 70°M for 700m, going quickly downhill. After going through the gate, pick up a path going directly downhill bearing 350°M from the gate, off the peak towards Humphrey Bottom. Take extreme care descending the steep steps. Follow the slabbed path from the base in the same general direction back to The Old Hill Inn.

It is important to re-state that all bearings given in these emergency descent routes are magnetic bearings, 3° having been already added.

Remember to inform Pen-y-ghent Café if you cannot get back to Horton and you have used the safety system. Should you be able

to reach a telephone somewhere then call 01729-860333 to inform them of your present position. In case of major problems dial 999 asking for cave rescue at Settle police station.

At night if you are lost but are warm and unhurt, try to go carefully on a path down to the lower slopes, off the peaks and out of the wind. Put on warm clothing and eat some food. Alternatively you can shelter out of the wind until daylight then establish your position before proceeding down to safety. A GPS is a modern aid to help you to establish your position.

Note: It is always advisable, particularly in this situation, to have with you the items recommended in the equipment list described earlier. In the modern age of technology, a mobile telephone may be of use in this situation, reception permitting.

Photo 20. Passing the farm at Bruntscar

Post Walk

Arriving back in Horton in Ribblesdale, return to the café to 'clock back in'. Ask for your card at the counter. People who complete the 3 peaks in less than 12 hours and 'clocked out/in' correctly are invited to join 'The 3 Peaks of Yorkshire Club'

The town of Settle is only a few miles away where there is the Fisherman's Rest fish and chip shop as well as a selection of public houses to cater for all tastes. There are two public bars in Horton.

Each year on the last Sunday in April, the 3 peaks race takes place. This obviously undulating and strenuous course takes around 2 hours and 30 minutes for the fastest athletes to complete. The race is run under strict rules and there is a limit of 200 runners on the set route. Perhaps those walkers who like more of a challenge may apply to enter the race!

After achieving your goal of walking the Yorkshire 3 Peaks, you may like a souvenir to mark the event. The author has produced a photo DVD of the full route on a slideshow with over 170 photos in full colour.

This will provide a lasting souvenir of your achievement. It can be viewed on a PC or on a television via a DVD player. Full details and prices are available on our website **www.chall-pub.co.uk**

Visit out National 3 Peaks website if you have walked or are planning to walk the National 3 Peaks. We produce an extensive list of souvenirs for the National 3 Peaks which are shown on the website: **www.national3peaks.co.uk**

Alternatively send for a current price list to:

Brian Smailes
Challenge Publications
7, Earlsmere Drive
Ardsley
Barnsley
South Yorkshire
S71 5HH

Items of Interest on Route

Within the village of Horton in Ribblesdale there are a number of amenities and places of interest.

Arriving in Horton, there is a large car park (charge) with public toilets situated close by. The famous Pen-y-ghent Café is just a short distance away. It is also a tourist information centre with books and walking equipment on sale.

Further along the road is Holme Farm Campsite. Walkers and backpackers frequently use this. Across the road is the local church, which is dedicated to St. Oswald and is generally of Norman Style, originally built in 1100's but modernised in the 1400's and again in Victorian times. This is worth a visit when passing.

The River Ribble runs through the village on its course and there are a number of bridges over it. After leaving the river on your left, you begin walking up the lower slopes leading to Pen-y-ghent. There are good views back towards Horton and the quarry beyond, also of Whernside and Ingleborough.

Proceed along the route and once over Pen-y-ghent summit you can see Ribblehead Viaduct in the distance and in the valley below Hull Pot, a well-known pothole. Walking towards Whernside, Ribblehead Viaduct can be seen

Photo 21. Crossing the fields just after leaving The Old Hill Inn

more clearly. Beneath the viaduct there is a monument and cairn dedicated to the building and subsequent restoration of the viaduct by British Rail and to those who built it between 1870 and 1875.

The viaduct has 24 arches and is 104ft high and 440yds long. Passing close to the viaduct by the railway line, you may see numerous steam train enthusiasts all armed with cameras who appear if a steam train is about to pass.

On the summit of Whernside there are spectacular views across to the west and Morecambe Bay as well as the mountains of the Lake District to the north, (weather permitting). In the valley between Whernside and Ingleborough there is a natural rest stop at the Old Hill Inn. This place provides good food and a wide selection of drinks. It is important to stress that alcohol consumed in quantity can be dangerous to the walker as it can give a false sense of security, as well as making you unsteady while walking.

On gaining the summit of Ingleborough you again have good views of Morecambe Bay and of the path to Horton in the opposite direction.

Overall, the scenery and open moorland views looking up to the peaks or down the valley are spectacular and well worth the effort attempting this circular walk.

Summer Flowers to be seen on route:

- *Oxeye*
- *Daisy*
- *Heather*
- *Daisy*
- *Dandelion*
- *White Clover*
- *Tufted Vetch*
- *Soft Rush*
- *Thorny Purple Thistle*
- *Harebell*
- *Common Vetch*
- *Willow Herb*
- *Primrose*
- *Meadow Thistle*
- *Buttercup*

Useful Information

Campsites

Holme Farm Campsite
Horton in Ribblesdale,
Settle, BD24 0HD
Tel 01729 860281

Knight
Stainforth Hall Caravan & Camping
Park, Little Stainforth, Settle,
BD24 0DP
Tel 01729 822200

Accommodation Selection

The following B&Bs have been chosen for their reasonable prices, comfort
and proximity to the start of the walk. They are not arranged in any order
of priority and you are advised to book in advance at busy holiday periods.
Please mention to the B&B that you have this book.

Broad Croft House,
Horton in Ribblesdale,
BD24 0EX
Tel. 01729 860302
www.broadcroft.co.uk
email on website.

Golden Lion Hotel,
Horton in Ribblesdale,
Settle, N. Yorks.
BD24 0HB
Tel 01729 860206
tricia@goldenlionhotel.co.uk
www.goldenlionhotel.co.uk

Bunk Room with 55-bunk capacity
C. Johnson,
1, Chapel Lane,
Horton in Ribblesdale, Settle,
N. Yorks. BD24 0HA
Tel 01729 860380
www.threepeaksbunkroom.co.uk

Station Inn,
Alan Shutt,
Ribblehead Viaduct,
Ingleton,
LA6 3AS,
Tel 015242 241274
www.thestationinn.net
info@thestationinn.net
*Bunk Barns, cheap & cheerful
with hotel rooms available.*

The Willows B&B
Hawes Road
Horton in Ribblesdale
BD24 0HT
Tel 01729 860200
www.the-willows-horton-in-ribblesdale.co.uk
johanne2@sky.com
Grid Ref. SD 804726

Heights of Peaks

Pen-y-ghent	694m.	2277ft.
Whernside	736m.	2414ft.
Ingleborough	723m.	2372ft.

Walking Times

From	To	Time
Horton in Ribblesdale	Pen-y-ghent Summit	1 hr 15 min.
Pen-y-ghent Summit	Ribblehead	2 hr 40 min.
Ribblehead	Force Gill	45 min
Force Gill	Whernside Summit	1 hr 00 min.
Whernside Summit	The Old Hill Inn	1 hr 15 min.
The Old Hill Inn	Ingleborough Summit	1 hr 30 min.
Ingleborough Summit	Horton in Ribblesdale	2 hr 10 min.

TOTAL 10hr 35 min.

Add extra time for breaks on route, size of party, weather conditions and fitness of group/individuals. It is advisable to start this walk around 6-9am and plan to finish before darkness.

Photo 22. The slabbed path to the base of Ingleborough

Photo 23. The short steep ascent here in snow with the evening sun backdrop

Distances to Nearest Main Villages (by most direct route)

From	To	Distance
Pen-y-ghent Summit	Horton	2.7 miles/4.4km.
Whernside Summit	Ingleton Village	7.1 miles/11.4km
Ingleborough Summit	Ingleton Village	3.4 miles/5.5km.
Ingleborough Summit	Horton	4.9 miles/ 7.9 km.

Other Notable Distances

From	To	Distance
Horton	Pen-y-ghent Summit	3.1 miles/5km.
Horton	Ribblehead	9.8 miles/15.8km
Ribblehead	Whernside Summit	3.4 miles/5.5km.
Ribblehead	Old Hill Inn Inn	7.5 miles/12.1 km.
Old Hill Inn Inn	Ingleborough Summit	2.5 miles/ 4 km.
Old Hill Inn Inn	Horton	7.6 miles/12.2 km.

Nearest Telephones on Route

Horton in Ribblesdale	- Car park entrance.
Horton in Ribblesdale Station	- Platform waiting room.
The Station Inn Pub	- Just up the road from Ribblehead Viaduct.
The Old Hill Inn (Porch)	- Checkpoint 2

Public Houses/Refreshments

Pen-y-ghent Café	Horton	The Station Inn	Ribblehead
The Crown Hotel	Horton	Philpin Snack Bar,	Chapel le Dale
Golden Lion Hotel	Horton	The Old Hill Inn	Chapel le Dale
Mobile Tea Bar	Ribblehead		

National Park Centres

The following National Park Centres will also be pleased to assist walkers and other visitors to the Dales with any queries.

Aysgarth Falls	01969 662910	Malham	01729 833200
Grassington	01756 751690	Reeth	01748 884059
Hawes	01969 666210		

Photo 24. The final push to the summit of Ingleborough with the turn off right, back to Horton by the small vertical stone

T.I.Cs in the 3 Peaks Area

Horton in Ribblesdale	01729 860333
Settle	01729 825192
Ingleton	01524 241049

All the T.I.Cs will be pleased to offer help and advice to ensure you enjoy your visit to the Yorkshire Dales.

Useful Addresses /Telephone Numbers

Friends of The Three Peaks - Yorkshire Dales

A group of individuals and organisations that want to care for the landscape and environment in the 3 peaks area.

c/o Josie Simpson,
Yorkshire Dales National Park Authority,
Colvend, Hebden Rd, Grassington,
Skipton, North Yorks
BD23 5LBv

Yorkshire Wildlife Trust

Tel: 01904 659570

Yorkshire Dales Society

Tel: 01729 825600

An independent charity, operating to protect, conserve and promote the dales

Photo 25. The 4 way wind shelter and 'trig' point on Ingleborough summit

Long Distance Walkers Association

Paul Lawrence,
15, Tamarisk Rise,
Wokingham,
Berkshire RG40 1WG

Tel 01189 790190

This association is set up to further the interests of those who enjoy long distance walking. Members receive a journal three times each year, (Strider), which includes information on all aspects of long distance walking.

Website: www.ldwa.org.uk

E-mail:LDP@ldwa.org.uk

Ramblers Association

2nd Floor,
Camelford House,
87-90, Albert Embankment,

London SE1 7TW

Tel. 0207 3398500

Advice and information on all walking matters. Local groups hold regular meetings.

Yorkshire Dales National Park Authority Bainbridge Headquarters

Tel: 0300 4560030

The authority helps look after the National Park, protecting its wildlife, natural beauty and cultural heritage whilst promoting opportunities for the understanding and enjoyment of the park.

Photo 26. The route back to Horton in the valley by the white houses

Glossary of Words

B&B - Bed and breakfast.

Bearing - A degree or number of degrees set on a compass then follow the direction of travel arrow to walk on that bearing to reach your intended destination.

Beck – A stream or brook.

Crag - A steep rugged rock or peak.

Dyke, Dike, Ditch - Words used to denote a long ridge of earth or a water channel either raised up or below normal level.

G.P.S. - Global Positioning System. Grid Reference - Derived from the National grid reference system. This is used to pinpoint a place on a map by the use of letters and numbers, written as GR. _ _ _ _ _ _

Kissing Gate - Swing gate that usually lets one person through it at a time by moving the gate backwards and forwards.

Magnetic Bearing - This is a grid bearing taken from a map and the relevant magnetic variation added to it to obtain the magnetic bearing. See the relevant maps for details of current magnetic variation.

Metalled Road - Generally known as a stone-chipping road. This term evolved and became known as the roads metal or the roads surface.

Outcrop - Part of a rock formation that protrudes from the main body of rock.

Path - A narrow path of grass, mud, stone etc. suitable for walkers. Not usually more than 2m wide.

Plateau - A wide and mainly flat area of elevated land.

Summit - The highest point of a mountain or hill.

Tarn - A small landlocked mountain lake.

T.I.C. - Tourist Information Centre.

Track - A road (possibly rough) usually wide enough for a vehicle and often leading to a farm. Usually more than 2m wide.

Trig Point - True name is triangulation pillar. These mark the summit of many mountains, but not every mountain has one. It is a small stone pillar with a number on it. The height of the mountain is taken from this point.

The route described in this book was used by the author in 2011 and believed to be correct at the time of publication. Hopefully you have enjoyed your 3 Peaks walk and gained as much pleasure from it as he did.

Should you wish to walk other challenging routes, please visit Challenge Publications web site at:

www.chall-pub.co.uk

Or the National 3 Peaks web site
www.national3peaks.co.uk

A wide selection of walking and other guides covering the UK are available including:

- The National 3 Peaks Walk
- Hadrian's Wall
- The Lyke Wake Walk
- John O'Groats to Lands End

These books, like the others produced contain everything you need to know to complete the challenge. See list in front of book.

On our website you will find other interesting, and possibly different walks around the British Isles, which are equally as picturesque and enjoyable as this one.

Should you wish to comment on this book or give further information to help keep the book updated then please write to the address below or e-mail via the website. An acknowledgement will be given.

**Challenge Publications
7, Earlsmere Drive
Ardsley, Barnsley
South Yorkshire
S71 5HH**

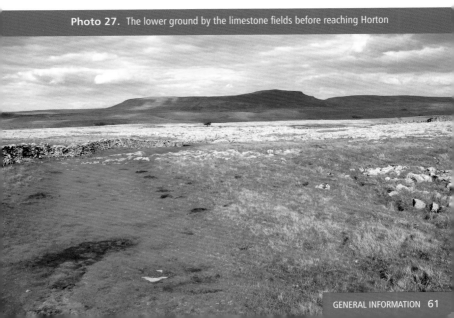

Photo 27. The lower ground by the limestone fields before reaching Horton

Photo 28. The signpost before reaching Horton with Pen-y-ghent in the background

SELSIDE · BW CLAPHAM 3¾ >

Notes

Photo 29. Horton ahead showing the path which crosses the fields